First World War
and Army of Occupation
War Diary
France, Belgium and Germany

57 DIVISION
171 Infantry Brigade
King's (Liverpool Regiment)
2/6 Battalion
20 September 1915 - 1 February 1916

WO95/2983/3

Published by

The Naval & Military Press Ltd

Unit 10 Ridgewood Industrial Park,

Uckfield, East Sussex,

TN22 5QE England

Tel: +44 (0) 1825 749494

www.naval-military-press.com

www.nmarchive.com

This diary has been reprinted in facsimile from the original. Any imperfections are inevitably reproduced and the quality may fall short of modern type and cartographic standards.

© **Crown Copyright**
Images reproduced by permission of The National Archives, London, England, 2015.

Contents

Document type	Place/Title	Date From	Date To
Heading	WO95/2983/3 57 Div, 171 Infantry Bde 2/6 Btn Kings Liverpool Regt Aug 1915-March 1916		
Miscellaneous	Summary Of 2/6th (Rifle) Battalion "The Kings" (Liverpool Regiment) For August 1915	03/09/1915	03/09/1915
Miscellaneous	2/6th (Rifle) Battalion "The Kings" (Liverpool Regt)	03/09/1915	03/09/1915
Heading	War Diary Of 2/6th (Rifle) Battalion "The King's" (Liverpool Regiment) From 1st September 1915 To 30th September 1915		
War Diary	Upstreet	20/09/1915	28/09/1915
Heading	2/6th (Rifle) Battalion "The King's" (Liverpool Regiment) War Diary From 1st October 1915 To 31st October 1915		
War Diary	Upstreet	04/10/1915	20/10/1915
War Diary	Canterbury	31/10/1915	31/10/1915
Heading	War Diary Of 2/6th (Rifle) Battalion "The King's" (Liverpool Regiment) From 1st November 1915 To 30th November 1915		
War Diary	Canterbury	01/11/1915	30/11/1915
Heading	War Diary Of The 2/6th (Rifle) Battalion "The King's" (Liverpool Regiment) Form 1st December 1915 To 31st December 1915		
War Diary	Canterbury	01/12/1915	31/12/1915
Heading	War Diary Of The 2/6th (Rifle) Battalion "The King's" (Liverpool Regiment) From 1st January 1916 To 31st January 1916		
War Diary	Canterbury	01/01/1916	31/01/1916
Heading	War Diary Of The 2/6th (Rifle) Battalion "The King's" (Liverpool Regiment) From 1st February 1916 To 29th February 1916		
War Diary	Canterbury	01/02/1916	29/01/1916

WO 95/2983/3

57 DIV, 171 INFANTRY BDE

2/6 Bn KING'S LIVERPOOL REGT

Aug 1915 - March 1916

CONFIDENTIAL.

SUMMARY

of

2/6th (RIFLE) BATTALION "THE KING'S" (LIVERPOOL REGIMENT).

for

AUGUST 1915.

Upstreet Camp,
   KENT.
3rd September 1915.

CONFIDENTIAL.

2/6th (RIFLE) BATTALION "THE KING'S" (LIVERPOOL REGT).

Headquarters:-
UPSTREET CAMP
3rd September 1915.

Brigade ... ... 171st Infantry Brigade,
Division ... ... 57th (West Lancashire) Division
Mobilization Centre.. Canterbury
Temporary War Station. Upstreet, Kent.

a & b. Unit formed after mobilization of T.F. had been ordered. Concentrated move from Blackpool to Canterbury, thence to Margate. On the 12th July 1915, the Battalion moved by march route to Upstreet Camp.

c. ORGANISATION FOR DEFENCE (INCLUDING VULNERABLE POINTS) On "Alarm" sounding the Battalion will fall in on Battalion Parade Ground and take such steps as circumstances demand. In the case of a raid by hostile aircraft special orders have been issued, the hedges round the camp being occupied. Ration for one day for each man ready for immediate issue. Transport to Q M.Stores.

AMMUNITION ON HAND.

	Practice.	Equipment.
New...	Nil	120,000.
Mark VI.	6,743.	10,000. (M.G)
Mark VII	Nil	Nil.

d. TRAINING. Coy. Training, Bayonet Fighting (including Final Assault practice) Route Marches with Transport, Musketry (including manual exercises and miniature), Physical Drill, Entrenching, Night Operations, Alarms (day & night), Extended Order Drill, Attack formations, Range Finding (with Merinden Range Finder), Outpost Practices, Brigade Manoeuvres, Lectures, Semaphore practice, Machine Gun, Signalling & Bomb throwing classes.
Note:- For some days the Battalion has been engaged on trench improvement work.

e. DISCIPLINE. The Discipline of the Battalion still remains good. We have had no D.C.M's this month.

f. ADMINISTRATION.

1. R.A.M.C., M.O. Sanitary Squad & R.A.M.C. Water Squad now fully employed.

2. Veterinary Services. Brigade Veterinary Officer attends sick horses as required, a Civilian Vet. only being employed by Brigade sanction in urgent cases.

3. Supply Services. Rations sent by A.S.C from Canterbury daily. Extra grocery ration supplied by proprietor of Canteen & Regimental Institute, Messrs H.M.Baker & Son, of Canterbury.

4. Transport Services. We have now received 19 mules but are without harness to use them.

5. Ordnance Services. Battalion now full equipped with 1914 equipment with the exception of 700 entrenching tools. The further materials necessary for camp comfort are coming forward slowly, but the work is in hand. We still have no Machine Gun.

2.

6. Billeting.   Battalion now under canvas.

7. Channels of Correspondence in Routine Matters.   All correspondence for higher authority referred to 171st Infantry Brigade, except Departmental correspondence, which is passed to the interested parties.

8. Range Construction.   Nearest open-air range - Sandwich. We have erected a miniature open-air range on the marshes.

9. Remounts.   We have now 14 Govt. owned Officers' Remounts.

g. REORGANISATION OF T.F. INTO HOME AND IMPERIAL SERVICE.

We ahave now only 31 Home Service men (Band) on strength, the remainder of the men having accepted the I.S obligation.

h. PREPARATION OF UNITS FOR I.S. The Unit is now attaining a high degree of efficiency and every effort is being made to make the Battalion ready to proceed on Service at an early date.

W A L Fletcher

Lieut. Colonel
Commanding   2/6th (Rifle) Battalion K.L.R.

C O N F I D E N T I A L.

W A R   D I A R Y

O F

2/6th.(RIFLE) BATTALION "THE KING'S" (LIVERPOOL REGIMENT)

    F R O M   1st. SEPTEMBER, 1915.
    T O   30th. SEPTEMBER, 1915.

UPSTREET CAMP,
  NEAR CANTERBURY.

3rd. October, 1915.

WAR DIARY
or
INTELLIGENCE SUMMARY.

(Erase heading not required.)

Army Form C. 2118.

Instructions regarding War Diaries and Intelligence Summaries are contained in F. S. Regs., Part II. and the Staff Manual respectively. Title pages will be prepared in manuscript.

Place	Date	Hour	Summary of Events and Information	Remarks and references to Appendices
Wyschaete	2nd Sept 1915		8 complete sets of Pack Saddlery received	
Wyschaete	5th Sept 1915		2nd Lieut (B.N. Osmond) 16th Bn. The King's (Liverpool Regt) Invalided from British Expeditionary Force, France) joined for duty	
Wyschaete	15th Sept 1915		Lieut R.J. Dowell (invalided from British Expeditionary Force, France) joined for duty	
Wyschaete	16th Sept 1915		The Battalion, under orders from G.O.C. 37th (Wet Lancs) Divn commenced defences improvement work at Imperial Army Trenches. Also all other training. 17 sets of harness were received on this date.	
Wyschaete	23rd Sept 1915		Major R. Wainwright (invalided from British Expeditionary Force, France) joined for duty	
Wyschaete	28th Sept 1915		4 Field Kitchens received	

West Stubbington Col.
Comdg 46 Rifle Bn K.L.R.

C O N F I D E N T I A L .

2/6th. (RIFLE) BATTALION "THE KING'S" (LIVERPOOL REGIMENT).

W A R   D I A R Y.

From 1st. October, 1915.

To 31st. October, 1915.

Canterbury,
    3rd. November, 1915.

Army Form C. 2118.

WAR DIARY
or
INTELLIGENCE SUMMARY.
(Erase heading not required.)

Instructions regarding War Diaries and Intelligence Summaries are contained in F. S. Regs., Part II. and the Staff Manual respectively. Title pages will be prepared in manuscript.

Place	Date	Hour	Summary of Events and Information	Remarks and references to Appendices
Upstreet	4th Oct. 1915		D.C.M. on No 3291 Pte N. Matchett held at Upstreet Camp.	
Upstreet	5th Oct 1915		6 Heavy Draught horses transferred to A.S.C. Canterbury. War Office instructions received through Brigade that there should be no firing at aeroplanes, hostile or otherwise.	
Upstreet	7th Oct. 1915		First Line Transport inspected by O.C. 5/? (100 s/nees) on Train.	
Upstreet	8th Oct 1915		Sentence of 14 days detention on Pte Matchett promulgated by O.C.M.	
Upstreet	9th Oct 1915		Instructions of 5th instant re Aircraft cancelled and original instructions reinstated.	
Upstreet	14th Oct 1915		D.C.M. on No. 3033 Pte J.P. Edwards held at Upstreet. Battalion inspected by representative of Ministry of Munitions. Two light Draught horses transferred to 2/5th Bn Liverpool Regt and one to 2/8th Bn Liverpool Regt.	

W. W. Fletcher Lt Col
(cont)

1577 Wt. W10791/1773 500,000 1/15 D. D. & L. A.D.S.S./Forms/C. 2118.

Army Form C. 2118.

WAR DIARY
or
INTELLIGENCE SUMMARY.
(Erase heading not required.)

Instructions regarding War Diaries and Intelligence Summaries are contained in F. S. Regs., Part II. and the Staff Manual respectively. Title pages will be prepared in manuscript.

Place	Date	Hour	Summary of Events and Information	Remarks and references to Appendices
Upstreet	15th Oct 1915	7.48 p.m.	Alarm sounded 7.48 p.m.	
Upstreet	17th Oct 1915		Sentence of 56 days detention by DCM on No. 3033 Rifleman J.P. Edwards promulgated.	
Upstreet	30th Oct 1915		Battalion moved by Route March to Billets in Canterbury.	
Canterbury	31st Oct 1915	8.50 A.M.	Alarm sounded 8.50 A.M.	

W.A.H. Fletcher Lt Col.

1577 Wt.W10791/1773 500,000 1/15 D. D. & L. A.D.S.S./Forms/C. 2118.

PRIVATE AND CONFIDENTIAL.

WAR DIARY

OF

2/5th. (RIFLE) BATTALION "THE KING'S" (LIVERPOOL REGIMENT).

FROM 1st. NOVEMBER, 1915.

TO 30th. NOVEMBER, 1915.

CANTERBURY.
3.12.15.

Army Form C. 2118

WAR DIARY
or
INTELLIGENCE SUMMARY
(Erase heading not required.)

Instructions regarding War Diaries and Intelligence Summaries are contained in F. S. Regs., Part II. and the Staff Manual respectively. Title Pages will be prepared in manuscript.

Place	Date	Hour	Summary of Events and Information	Remarks and references to Appendices
Canterbury	1/11/15		Inauguration of Machine Gun Section as a separate unit under 2nd Lieut. J.C.B Ewing.	JB
do.	2/11/15		Nil.	JB
do.	3/11/15		Inauguration of Pioneer Section.	JB
do.	4/11/15		Brigade Field Operations	JB
do.	5/11/15		Nil	JB
do.	6/11/15		Nil	JB
do.	7/11/15		Nil	JB
do.	8/11/15		Battalion commanders being Long but Short Route March. Battalion furnished advance Guard of 1 Officer and — ranks to Column.	JB
do.	9/11/15		Horses No. 47 and 69 transferred to 171st Infantry Brigade.	JB
do.	10/11/15		Nil	JB
do.	11/11/15 (cont)		Battalion participated in Brigade Field Operations	JB

Army Form C. 2118

WAR DIARY
or
INTELLIGENCE SUMMARY
(Erase heading not required.)

Instructions regarding War Diaries and Intelligence Summaries are contained in F. S. Regs., Part II. and the Staff Manual respectively. Title Pages will be prepared in manuscript.

Place	Date	Hour	Summary of Events and Information	Remarks and references to Appendices
Canterbury	11/11/15		Horses Nos 1 and 5 exchanged with 3/5th Bn Lincolnshire Regt for horses 21 and 43. Horses Nos. 41, 169, 173 and 194 (Riding) transferred to R.F.A. at ASH. Horses Nos 21 and 43 (Light Draught) and mules O1 and O31 transferred to R.F.A. at ASH. Horses 28 and 57 (Heavy Draught) transferred to A.S.C. 57th (but Lance) Divn. on 12th Nov. 1915.	JB
do	12/11/15		Nil	JM
	13/11/15		Nil	JB
	14/11/15		Nil	JB
	15/11/15		Nil	JB
	16/11/15		157,000 rounds of .303 ammunition received	JB
	17/11/15		Nil	JB
	18/11/15		First line transport paraded for inspection by General Langhow, but inspection was cancelled	JB
	19/11/15		Nil	JB
	20/11/15		525 .303 Rifles received.	JB
	21/11/15		Japanese arms and ammunition returned to Woolwich	JB

WAR DIARY
or
INTELLIGENCE SUMMARY

(Erase heading not required.)

Army Form C. 2118

Place	Date	Hour	Summary of Events and Information	Remarks and references to Appendices
Canterbury	22/11/15		Acting on instructions dining Ch. of Officers reduced to 23 (Infantry) minimum establishment for 2nd Line T.F. units) Surplus posted to 3rd Line.	J.B. /9/13
do	23/11/15		52,500 rounds of .303 ammunition despatched to Divisional Supply Column.	9/13
do	24/11/15		Battalion inspected by Inspector General of Infantry, whose comments were very favourable.	J.B.
do	25/11/15		Nil.	1/2
do	26/11/15		S.C.M. on No.3291 Rfn W. Wiggins held at 6th Batty. Canterbury.	2/13 9/13
do	27/11/15		Battalion furnishes detachment of 2 Officers and 75 men for Coast defence duties at Sheerness.	9/13
do	28/11/15		Sentence by S.C.M. of 56 days detention on No.3291 Rfn to orig. ino promulgated.	9/13
do	29/11/15		Nil	1/A
do	30/11/15		Nil	1/A

Cbury
1-12-15

H. Kerr Wilson
Major
Comdg 2/6 (Rifle) Bn Liverpool Regt.

1875 Wt. W593/826 1,000,000 4/15 J.B.C. & A. A.D.S.S./Forms/C. 2118.

CONFIDENTIAL.

WAR DIARY.

OF THE

2/6th.(RIFLE) BATTALION "THE KING'S" (LIVERPOOL REGIMENT)

FROM   1st.DECEMBER, 1915.
TO   31st.DECEMBER, 1915.

CANTERBURY.
3.1.16.

Army Form C. 2118

WAR DIARY
or
INTELLIGENCE SUMMARY
(Erase heading not required.)

Instructions regarding War Diaries and Intelligence Summaries are contained in F. S. Regs., Part II. and the Staff Manual respectively. Title Pages will be prepared in manuscript.

Place	Date	Hour	Summary of Events and Information	Remarks and references to Appendices
Canterbury	1st Dec 1915		NIL	JB
"	2nd Dec 1915		Battalion took part in Brigade Field operations. Alarm sounded 9.50 p.m.	JB
"	3rd Dec 1915		1st line Transport inspected at O.C Park Canterbury by the No. 3 Coy. O.C (2nd Lancs) Brit. Trans. of G.S. — Transport officer advised that horse in possession was for drawing G.S. wagons mark X were too light. Application accordingly made for heavier horses.	M
"	4th Dec 1915		NIL	JB
"	5th Dec 1915		NIL	JB
"	6th Dec 1915		NIL	JB
"	7th Dec 1915		NIL	JB

W/Col Arthur Stone

1875 Wt. W593/826 1,000,000 4/15 J.B.C. & A. A.D.S.S./Forms/C. 2118.

Army Form C. 2118

WAR DIARY
or
INTELLIGENCE SUMMARY
(Erase heading not required.)

Instructions regarding War Diaries and Intelligence Summaries are contained in F.S. Regs., Part II. and the Staff Manual respectively. Title Pages will be prepared in manuscript.

Place	Date	Hour	Summary of Events and Information	Remarks and references to Appendices
Canterbury	8th Dec 1915		NIL	
do.	9th Dec 1915		Battalion participates in Brigade Field Operations	
do.	10th Dec 1915		Alarm Sounded 10.30 pm.	
do.	11th Dec 1915		Application for heavy draught horses for G S wagons March & return to be Submitted 18th December	
do.	12th Dec 1915		NIL	
do.	13th Dec 1915		NIL	
do.	14th Dec 1915		NIL	
do.	15th Dec 1915		NIL	

1875 Wt. W593/826 1,000,000 4/15 J.B.C. & A. A.D.S.S./Forms/C. 2118.

Army Form C. 2118

WAR DIARY
or
INTELLIGENCE SUMMARY
(Erase heading not required.)

Instructions regarding War Diaries and Intelligence Summaries are contained in F. S. Regs., Part II. and the Staff Manual respectively. Title Pages will be prepared in manuscript.

Place	Date	Hour	Summary of Events and Information	Remarks and references to Appendices
Canterbury	16th Dec 1915		NIL	JB
"	17th Dec 1915		NIL	JB
"	18th Dec 1915		Application for heavy draught horses for G.S. wagons Mark x x submitted	JB
"	19th Dec 1915		Application for heavy draught horses returned with comment that as the unit is shortly to be oversea which 58 (number) wagons mark x would not be required.	JB
"	20th Dec 1915		NIL	JB
"	21st Dec 1915		Heavy snowed 2 p.m.	JB

Walter Arthur Little

1875 Wt. W593/826 1,000,000 4/15 J.B.C. & A. A.D.S.S./Forms/C. 2118.

WAR DIARY
or
INTELLIGENCE SUMMARY

(Erase heading not required.)

Army Form C. 2118

Instructions regarding War Diaries and Intelligence Summaries are contained in F. S. Regs., Part II. and the Staff Manual respectively. Title Pages will be prepared in manuscript.

Place	Date	Hour	Summary of Events and Information	Remarks and references to Appendices
Canterbury	22/12/15		NIL	[sig]
do	23/12/15		NIL	[sig]
do	24/12/15		Half Holiday	[sig]
do	25/12/15		Xmas Day	[sig]
do	26/12/15		NIL	[sig]
do	27/12/15		Holiday	[sig]
do	28/12/15		NIL	[sig]
do	29/12/15		NIL	[sig]

1875 Wt. W593/826 1,000,000 4/15 J.B.C. & A. A.D.S.S./Forms/C. 2118.

Army Form C. 2118

WAR DIARY
or
INTELLIGENCE SUMMARY

(Erase heading not required.)

Instructions regarding War Diaries and Intelligence Summaries are contained in F. S. Regs., Part II. and the Staff Manual respectively. Title Pages will be prepared in manuscript.

Place	Date	Hour	Summary of Events and Information	Remarks and references to Appendices
Canterbury	30/12/15	NIL		JB
do.	31/12/15	NIL	West Station 2 pl oc.	JB

1875 Wt. W593/826 1,000,000 4/15 J.B.C. & A. A.D.S.S./Forms/C. 2118.

CONFIDENTIAL.

WAR DIARY.

OF THE

2/6th.(RIFLE) BATTALION "THE KING'S" (LIVERPOOL REGIMENT).

FROM 1st. JANUARY, 1916.

TO 31st. JANUARY, 1916.

CANTERBURY.

1st. FEBRUARY, 1916.

Army Form C. 2118

WAR DIARY
or
INTELLIGENCE SUMMARY

(Erase heading not required.)

Instructions regarding War Diaries and Intelligence Summaries are contained in F. S. Regs., Part II. and the Staff Manual respectively. Title Pages will be prepared in manuscript.

Place	Date	Hour	Summary of Events and Information	Remarks and references to Appendices
Canterbury	1st Jany 1916		NIL	JB
do	2nd Jany 1916		Sniping School inaugurated.	JB
do	3rd Jany 1916		NIL	JB
do	4th Jany 1916		Battalions inspected in succession of Companies by G.O.C. II Army, Central Force.	JB
do	5th Jany 1916		NIL	JB
do	6th Jany 1916		NIL	JB
do	7th Jany 1916		NIL	JB

Col J Arthur Hose
Comdg 3/6 (Rifle) Bn Suffolk R

1875 Wt. W593/826 1,000,000 4/15 J.B.C. & A. A.D.S.S./Forms/C. 2118.

Army Form C. 2118

WAR DIARY
or
INTELLIGENCE SUMMARY
(Erase heading not required.)

Instructions regarding War Diaries and Intelligence Summaries are contained in F. S. Regs., Part II. and the Staff Manual respectively. Title Pages will be prepared in manuscript.

Place	Date	Hour	Summary of Events and Information	Remarks and references to Appendices
Canterbury	8/1/16		LIEUT. L.A. WILSON R A M C (T) took over duties of medical officer to this Battalion vice CAPTAIN J. LIVINGSTON R A M C (T)	JB
do	9/1/16		NIL	JB
do	10/1/16		NIL	JB
do	11/1/16		NIL	JB
do	12/1/16		NIL	JB
do	13/1/16		NIL	JB
do	14/1/16		Coast Defence Detachment at Buckingham withdrawn.	JB
do	15/1/16		NIL	JB
do	16/1/16		NIL	JB

Capt Arthur Hope
Comdg 2/6 (Reserve) Bn Queens R

1875 Wt. W593/826 1,000,000 4/15 J.B.C. & A. A.D.S.S./Forms/C. 2118.

Army Form C. 2118.

WAR DIARY
or
INTELLIGENCE SUMMARY.
(Erase heading not required.)

Instructions regarding War Diaries and Intelligence Summaries are contained in F. S. Regs., Part II. and the Staff Manual respectively. Title pages will be prepared in manuscript.

Place	Date	Hour	Summary of Events and Information	Remarks and references to Appendices
Canterbury	17/1/16		NIL	JB
Do	18/1/16		NIL	JB
Do	19/1/16		NIL	JB
Do	20/1/16		NIL	JB
Do	21/1/16		Received draft of 36 Recruits from Administrative Centre	JB
Do	22/1/16		Draft of 30 Recruits received	JB
Do	23/1/16		NIL	JB

Cox Arthur 2 Lt OC
Comdg 1/4 Hylds Mtd Bde MR

1577 Wt.W10791/1773 500,000 1/15 D. D. & L. A.D.S.S./Forms/C. 2118.

Army Form C. 2118

WAR DIARY
or
INTELLIGENCE SUMMARY

(Erase heading not required.)

Instructions regarding War Diaries and Intelligence Summaries are contained in F.S. Regs., Part II. and the Staff Manual respectively. Title Pages will be prepared in manuscript.

Place	Date	Hour	Summary of Events and Information	Remarks and references to Appendices
Canterbury	24/1/16	9 am	Practice alarm sounded 3 pm	JB
do	25/1/16		Draft of 35 recruits received	JB
do	26/1/16		Draft of 16 recruits received	JB
do	27/1/16		Draft of 10 recruits received	JB
do	28/1/16		Draft of 3 recruits received	JB
do	29/1/16		Draft of 4 recruits received	JB
do	30/1/16		NIL	JB
do	31/1/16	9 am	Practice alarm sounded 9.50 am	JB

W.A. Harding Lt Col
Comdg 4/1 (City of London) R.F.

1875 Wt. W593/826 1,000,000 4/15 J.B.C. & A. A.D.S.S./Forms/C. 2118.

CONFIDENTIAL

WAR DIARY

OF THE

2/6th.(RIFLE) BATTALION "THE KING'S" (LIVERPOOL REGIMENT)

FROM   1st. FEBRUARY, 1916.

TO   29th. FEBRUARY, 1916.

CANTERBURY.

1st. MARCH, 1916.

Army Form C. 2118

WAR DIARY
or
INTELLIGENCE SUMMARY

(Erase heading not required.)

Instructions regarding War Diaries and Intelligence Summaries are contained in F. S. Regs., Part II. and the Staff Manual respectively. Title Pages will be prepared in manuscript.

Place	Date	Hour	Summary of Events and Information	Remarks and references to Appendices
Canterbury	1/3/16		NIL	JB
do	2/3/16		NIL	JB
do	3/3/16		NIL	JB
do	4/3/16		NIL	JB
do	5/3/16		NIL	JB
do	6/3/16		NIL	JB
do	7/3/16		NIL	JB
do	8/3/16		NIL	JB

1875 Wt. W593/826 1,000,000 4/15 J.B.C. & A. A.D.S.S./Forms/C. 2118.

WAR DIARY
or
INTELLIGENCE SUMMARY

(Erase heading not required.)

Army Form C. 2118

Instructions regarding War Diaries and Intelligence Summaries are contained in F. S. Regs., Part II. and the Staff Manual respectively. Title Pages will be prepared in manuscript.

Place	Date	Hour	Summary of Events and Information	Remarks and references to Appendices
Cambrai	9/7/16		NIL	JR
do	1/9/16		NIL	JR
do	11/9/16		NIL	JR
do	2/9/16		NIL	JR
do	3/9/16		NIL	JR
do	4/9/16		NIL	JR
do	5/9/16		NIL	JR
do	10/9/16		NIL	JR
do	11/9/16		State of 18 recruits received from Immobilière Cadre	JR
do	9/9/16		NIL	JR

J. West Phillips Lt Col
Comdg 7th Reg'te Air Res N.R.

WAR DIARY
or
INTELLIGENCE SUMMARY
(Erase heading not required.)

Army Form C. 2118

Instructions regarding War Diaries and Intelligence Summaries are contained in F. S. Regs., Part II. and the Staff Manual respectively. Title Pages will be prepared in manuscript.

Place	Date	Hour	Summary of Events and Information	Remarks and references to Appendices
Canterbury	19/4/16		Practice Alarm G.P.S. gun.	JB
do	20/4/16		NIL	JB
do	21/4/16		NIL	JB
do	22/4/16		NIL	JB
do	23/4/16		NIL	JB
do	24/4/16		Received orders 11.10am - Prepare to move at moment's notice. Companies recalled from training. Ordered recalled 2.30, men to be allowed an hour for dinner. All ready to move off at 2.30 pm. Reported accordingly to Brigade Headquarters. Message received 4.50 pm. men 2 Coys in Zillebeke trenches failed to proceed to men at Belgian Hotel. Later instructed recruits training to be carried out incessantly of Zillebeke until further notice.	JB
do	25/4/16		State of readiness continued. Training carried on in vicinity of Brigade 6.15 pm. message received - Stand by ready to move off at an hour's notice.	JB
do	26/4/16		Training continued in vicinity of Zillebeke. Battalion stood by all day ready to move off.	JB

War Diary
April 1916 (Maps 19&20)
Lieut Col [signature]

Army Form C. 2118

WAR DIARY
or
INTELLIGENCE SUMMARY
(Erase heading not required.)

Instructions regarding War Diaries and Intelligence Summaries are contained in F. S. Regs., Part II. and the Staff Manual respectively. Title Pages will be prepared in manuscript.

Place	Date	Hour	Summary of Events and Information	Remarks and references to Appendices
Ambleurie	27/9/16		Battalion Stood by all day ready to move off.	JB
Do	28/9/16		Battalion Still Standing by	JB
Do	29/9/16		Battalion Still Standing by	JB
				Evan Fletcher Lt Col. Comdg 7th (Sprs) Bn Liverpool Regt

1875. Wt. W593/826 1,000,000 4/15 J.B.C. & A. A.D.S.S./Forms/C. 2118.